I0163303

SOUL STUFF

SOUL STUFF

How I used poetry and art to unlock all the gloriously raw and beautifully unbeautiful soul stuff stirring within.

Bryetta Calloway

Copyright © 2014 by Bryetta Calloway

All rights reserved. No part of this publication may be reproduced, distributed, or transmitted in any form or by any means, including photocopying, recording, or other electronic or mechanical methods, without the prior written permission of the publisher, except in the case of brief quotations embodied in critical reviews and certain other noncommercial uses permitted by copyright law. For permission requests, email to the publisher, addressed "Attention: Permissions Coordinator," at the address below.

info@bryetta.com

ISBN - 978-0-692-27688-4

Ordering Information:
For details, contact the publisher at the address above. Orders by U.S. trade bookstores and wholesalers. Please contact via address above or visit www.fedfull.com or www.bryetta.com.

Printed in the United States of America

For my mom, Lillian,
warrior, philosopher, and BFF

BRYETTA CALLOWAY is a singer, actress, speaker, and writer. She is the creator of fedFULL Living, an online community dedicated to empowering women to live fully and wholly. As a speaker she has traveled nationally speaking to organizations, churches, businesses, and communities.

As an actress and singer, Bryetta has performed on stages nationally and internationally. Her newly released EP, Fly Away, is currently available anywhere music is sold.

At 17, Bryetta attended New York University's, Tisch School of the Arts. As a student at CAP21 (Collaborative Arts Project 21) she studied musical theatre working with and studying under talented actors, directors, and choreographers. It is at NYU and the surrounding Greenwich Village she loves so much, that she began the process of integrating multiple artistic mediums to create new and fresh artistic perspectives. Prior to and since graduating from NYU, Bryetta has traveled the world performing. This global influence, merged with her love for the written word, and music has become the foundation of her artistic endeavors.

For more information about Bryetta and the projects she is currently working on visit www.bryetta.com or on Twitter at @Its_Bryetta.

contents

Introduction

I remember in elementary school falling off the monkey bars. Never truly physically inclined, I had been slowly tackling the seemingly never-ending two feet from side to side. I ran out to the bars, the recess button unlocking the beast within. I jumped up on the first bar and somewhere between bar one and two I got overconfident and slipped. Don't laugh, it happens to the best of us! Falling backward I hit my back on the metal bar acting as the highest step leading up to the bars. I knocked the wind out of myself and began to scream at the top of my lungs. That feeling, one I'll never forget, of the air, forced from my lungs started to overwhelm me. Immediately gasping and panicking to breathe, I was screaming out lung rattling screeches. My teacher ran over to me, grabbing my arms, yelling at me to breathe. Tears streaming down my face, I gasped out like a puckered fish on land, "I…can't…breathe…" over and over. Finally, my teacher frantically patting my back yelled in my tear stained face, a phrase I have never, ever forgotten. "If you can scream, you can breathe, now BREATHE!" I am sure it was not meant to be a thought shifting phrase, more likely an attempt to stop my mother from coming down there and raising a holy ruckus. However, through the years, that phrase has popped back up in my mind periodically. An ever-constant reminder that if, for one moment, I can abate the panic I can indeed breathe through what is threatening to suffocate me.

Recently, this phrase floated back through my subconscious again. Having completed another day working in the world's worst company, (don't try to fight me for this title, trust me, mine is worse than yours, so I win) I was at my emotional threshold. Dealing with a day filled with mean girls (dressed up as women), insults (veiled as questioning concern), side eyes (following my every movement) and schemes (poorly planned and even more poorly executed) had brought me to the place of, enough is enough. I found myself, much like I often had for the past several months, sitting on my mother's couch yelling at the top of my lungs, venting frustration. A daily exercise in white knuckling it through the day, holding in my pure thoughts, responses, and gut reactions had left me beyond words (a rarity for me, I assure you.) As I sat there, the fifth day in a row, the seventh week straight, complaining, ranting, and raving I finally ran out of words. I wanted nothing more than to have a full-on temper tantrum. The kind that is reminiscent of a five-year-old me, middle of the grocery store, NO I WANT THAT CEREAL, kind of temper tantrum. It was an intimidating feeling, this running out of things to say. Past comprehension, I had one of those rare moments we have in life where the words come tumbling out of us. Words that skirt past intellect and rationale and just pour straight from our souls, to our lips, right into the ears of God. Questions jumped up from inside me that asked, why did it have to be so hard, was money even worth this, how much longer was I expected to take this?

Completely husked and raw, I wiped the snot from my nose, my eyes puffy and red. Somehow, I had begun to access that stuff that brews deep down in the very private corners of your soul. The thoughts, utterances, and prayers you dare not voice in front of others, for fear they'd judge, mock, or even worse try to tell you how to fix it. My soul stuff was an amalgamation of fear, rage, hope, and love. The complicated stuff fraught with raw and unvarnished authentic truth. At this moment, I could hear my teacher running across the playground and dropping to her knees beside me and saying, "If you can scream, you can breathe." While the emotions were real, they were not the most important truth at that moment. What became all at once clear was that somehow in the process of daily living, I had stifled myself. So suffocated myself that it took all of this to get to the truth of what I was feeling. Spending so much time trying to be strong had masked the fact that I felt weak. Like many believers, I was guilty of the placebo effect of saying, "I'm okay" when in fact I was in desperate need. Not asking for help because no one wants to make God look bad! The responsibility I felt to portray that all is well was preventing God from unveiling the real beauty of the grace that had been afforded to me. The limited

13

abilities in me, or my family, or friends could not answer this kind of need. I needed a complete soul restoration. A system reboot and it required that I have a factory reset from my manufacturer because in the end, "I couldn't do this anymore."

I often laugh at God's awesome sense of humor. He knew exactly what he was doing when he gave me my mom. My mother is by career a mental health counselor, in life a spiritual warrior. Decades spent dragging homeless, incarcerated, addicted, traumatized, and broken women from the very edge were the reservoir from which I could draw. In that way that only those who deal with the broken on a daily basis can do, she spoke to me, her voice able to penetrate through the sniffles, the moans, and the guttural cries. She said to me, "Now, THAT'S, how you actually feel." Like one soothes a cornered animal she explained that anger was an easy emotion to reach for when too intimidated to label it truthfully as hurt, betrayal, and sadness. Just like the mom job description outlines, she spoke encouragement and quite frankly peace into my soul. Enough so, that as I walked away from her still sitting in the living room, my mind was racing with a new burning realization. I had begun to censor myself so brutally that I was suffering from a spiritual amnesia of sorts. My career is built on the ability to access the emotional truth of life. As a singer, actress, and writer it was easy for me to pull from those emotional places on demand but somehow in the process of everyday life, I had gotten muted. I could blame it on the hideous day job I was working to pay bills between gigs and late night recording sessions but the truth was it was more than that. As a person who prides herself on taking the time to truly assess how I feel and what I feel I had overlooked that pieces of myself were starving for replenishment.

Despite daily devotionals and church services, I had become spiritually muted. In true first born child order, type A personality activity (see mom I've been listening) I made a plan. I decided to take a concentrated period of time to actively listen to myself. So I made the commitment to dedicate 45 days to peeling back to a deeper level of listening. Not just the outpouring of my heart but the in-pouring of what God was trying to tell me. What came pouring out would be the meat and bones of this book. The words came out freely and once I began listening, like a bubbling brook it just kept flowing. As an artist, I spend a lot of my time writing music, reading scripts, and

14

speaking in front of audiences. So words are second nature to me. I've been a lover of language my entire life. The kind of kid that begged for extra trips to the library so that she could check out tons and tons of books. I consumed them like food, they fed me in a way those other things simply couldn't. And this is how I birthed fedfull.com a website dedicated to sharing in the language of encouragement and engaging other people (through the written word, music, and art) in a conversation about what is needed to live life fully. And so, as I was on this 45-day journey towards accessing more fully all of the stuff that stays locked in the deep recesses of our souls, these writings became my line of demarcation in the sand. A marker I would not let life push me past a certain point. I engaged in a battle to defend the mental and emotional freedom that is the blood right of all Christ believers. I embarked on that journey online through my website and Facebook page to share with others the journey I was on to begin to live more fully. These writings allowed my to pour out not just my own soul's "stuff" but to pen issues that, while I have not battled, burden so many broken believers.

My invitation to you as you journey through Soul Stuff is to take the time to sit down and access your own stuff. The things that you're afraid to say out loud. In my case, all the things that are simmering below the surface desperately screaming to be manifested were (for me) easily accessed through language, music or art. Your soul stuff may come in a different form than mine did. As I began to journal on a daily basis, it seemed that the words flowed out like poetry. I remember having a conversation with my sister about halfway through the 45 days that I had forgotten how much I loved poetry. I had forgotten how much I used to rely on writing poetry to express myself. I had honestly forgotten parts of myself intrinsic to who I was at the core. So as you read, make the commitment to journey through your own soul stuff. Do not be encumbered by the packaging of my stuff but, be genuine and authentic to how yours may be manifested. Whether scribbled on a torn receipt or notes in your phone, delve deeper.

So welcome to it, welcome to all the stuff that was bubbling beneath the surface of this singer, actress, and artist who forgot how to access all of the gloriously, messy, raw, and beautifully unbeautiful soul stuff that was locked within. May it give you permission to unlock yours.

welcome

Searching

Painfully stretching out from panic
I look for you.
You're everywhere
yet hidden at the same time.
I reach for you,
dazed and hungry
desperate for the
connection that you bring.
Meals salted with tears,
drinks shaken with fear.
My heart trembles,
my hands shake,
I am desperate for you.
I can't seem to see you
or summon your feel,
and so I stagger to the place
where you once were and kneel.
Chest heaving,
eyes blinking,
parched lips murmuring your name.
I wait for you here,
desperately longing.

Trust

Through the winding roads
of uncertainty,
I will trust you.
When life seems unfair
and uncompromising,
I will trust you.
When the mess of my life
hides the beauty of your face,
I will trust you.
When darkness reigns
and pain consumes,
I will trust you.
When intellect fails me
and speech does stall,
I will trust you.
When my mind is numb
and my heart is bound,
I will trust you.
There can be no other way
for fear to leave
and love to enter in.
I will trust you
even when I can't trace you.
I will trust you

even when I can't feel you.
I will trust you
because I love you.
And that love is all I need.

comforter

Comforter

My hands clutched tightly with yours
I am relieved with the connection.
A life spent alone and wandering
searching for protection.

I rest in the comfort
that you will always be near.
It wraps all around me
like the softest of cashmere.

Mine supple and vibrant
yours wizened with time,
there is beauty in our difference
it surpasses the sublime.

Like the arms of a lover or
mother and child,
you are all things to me
I am forever beguiled.

You are my sweet comforter
my shelter from the rain.
You soothe me when I'm wounded
you share with me my pain.

I am stronger for your presence.
I am greater for your embrace.
I beg that we never
leave this place.

Matchless

Your love is matchless
and consuming,
lovely and moving.
You have shown me
the reality of love,
in all of its messy,
forgiving,
exalting,
and shaping beauty.
I will breathe in all that you give
and use it to fuel my heart.
The greatest gift I have for you
is to rest
in the knowledge of your love.
Never doubting the authenticity
of your pledge to me.
I will settle into the embrace
of your touch.
You are home to me,
thank you
for leaving the light on.

Reconciliation

I want to find reconciliation
between who I am
and who I want to be.
I want to invite a conversation
between me now
and the me I'm yet to see.
I want no separation
between time now,
time then,
and time soon.
So I standstill in this moment
breathing,
hoping,
and believing
that three will become one
fractured will become whole
and I will be me;
then, now, and to be.

The Race

With lungs pumping
and arms flailing
I am running fast to find you.

Not certain where I'm destined
or what's ahead.
Your voice is summoning to
run, girl run.

I stumble over hurdles
that pop up along the way.
My stride is not pretty
gangly to see.

Bumpy and steep is the path
that leads to where you are.
On instinct alone,
I traverse the terrain.

The liquid of my flesh
is melting away as I race forward.
It is painful and cleansing, at once.

A baptism in motion
I am wet and being made new

as I go.
I am eager to see where it leads.

Thankful

I
love the   way you
love me, and   I'm awed by
the way you care.   There is something
infinitely consuming about knowing you
are always there. Because my past has
painfully taught me that love ebbs and
rarely flows, but there you are with love
so abundant that it forever grows and
grows.   So in the quiet of this
moment I want to take the
time to say, I thank you for
your loving me more
and more each
day.

Consuming

Overwhelmingly surrounding and
all together consuming
is your love for me.
You saved me from myself
for yourself.
There can be no other way
for love to grow than
to be submerged and enveloped
in your kindness.
I stumble upon explanation;
there is neither rhythm nor
rhyme to this love.
It is crazy and unpredictable
and yet I count on it
as if it were the air I breathe.
There is no equal
there can be no counterfeit
your love for me is matchless
I stand in awe.

Loveliness

The search for loveliness continues
it is so hard to find.
They that want to lift you up
not drag you through the grapevine.
They huddle in darkened corners,
they bring no joy or mirth.
Their tongues are like poisoned daggers
killing creativity before its birthed.

I am saddened by their sadness
their hatred a magnetic pull.
I fight to maintain gladness
and never let my heart go dull.

They feed on despair and chaos.
There is no unity here.
Like three hags around a cauldron
mumbling incantations to incite fear.

But inside me is the LOVELY ONE
with a love that pours and flows
that fills me with a power
no man could truly know.

Less he supped with the Master
and dined at HIS feet.
So I set my face before Him,
and lay my head to His heartbeat.

Like tears raining from heaven
to drown out the heat and fire,
He is my lovely one,
our love will never expire.

out of control

Out of Control

She is out-of-control
spinning wildly about,
sinking ever deeper
no way to come out.

She spends all her money
on music and drink.
Drowning out sorrow
not having to think.

She is chasing euphoria,
chasing the high.
Falling on her knees
desperate to try,
anything and anyone
that will make her forget.

That the life she is living
sinks her in debt.
Not just with the money
and not just with the things,
but also to her addictions

the ones she's made king.

She serves all her demons
they rule her mind.
She's lost in the circus
the creation of her own kind.

She bobs and weaves
trying to stand tall.
Yet the beauty of her spirit
continues to grow small.

Like a marionette on strings
she's jerked and pulled.
She dances to the beat
until the lights grow cool.

A synthetic happiness
a false sense of joy.
This is what it feels like
for a human yet broken toy.

She is out of control
spinning, whirling around.
She's dying in the crowd
not making a sound.

She spins on the barstool,
through the noise hearing her name.

The whisper of freedom promising change.

It woos her through the masses
and across the dance floor.
It pulls her to the lobby
and right out the door.

It leads her to the altar
and forces her to her knees.
Not knowing what to ask for
she simply says, "Please?"

Through the smell of the liquor
the day-old cologne
the sweet smell of Salvation
beckons her home.

Back to the Jesus she heard of as a child.
Back to the Savior before she went wild.

Mascara running
hair matted to her face,
the story of an out-of-control girl's
fall into grace.

Chasing

In shadows and in sleep do you come to me,
whispering through the corners of my mind.
In quietness and in sleep do you call out to me,
in the secrets of my heart do you reside.
There is room for you here in my spirit;
there is space for you here in my life.
Out of darkness and out of pain
did you pursue me,
and with you as my love
there is no strife.

You love it adds no sorrow,
your love it adds no pain,
and forever I will chase you,
calling out your name.

Love, oh love how you found me,

a mess, alone,
and afraid.
When I saw no value in my being,
the ultimate price did you pay.

You taught me with your faithfulness,
there can be no love without trade.
Your life for my love,
my place for your blood.
Without you,
life would never be the same.

Raging

Like a clarion call,
and the trumpet of war,
I shift my head to look out.

The battle is raging
and the call is made
there is chaos all about.

I can hide no longer in girlhood
the woman's war I have been called to fight.

So I stand on the field with my sisters,
weight shifting left to right.

The sword of truth in my hand,
determination and will in my face.

I lock my knees to brace me
as my pounding heart begins to race.

The time for dolls and games has ended;
there is a battle to be played.

For where one woman lacks her voice
then the move of change must rage.

You cannot escape your calling;
you're called as a daughter of war,
for the battles that you see around you
are asking you to do more.

For you are the solution
that we've been waiting for,
the answer to the problems we see.

The war of poverty, genocide and ignorance
is calling out to me.

To stand on the front lines of change
to release my battle cry.

I am a woman daughter of war,
and for this cause I will rise.

Destruction

The way of destruction
is not darkened and dank
not dirty and perverted
like you've been told to think.

Wide and accommodating
with beautiful sights to see.
The way to destruction
always beckoning.
It provides with friendship,
laughter, and mirth.
You can travel for years
before you unearth,
the baggage you picked up
along the trek.
So heavy and ladened
you long to turn back.

The path of destruction
has taken you far,
so distant from the person
you truly are.
For somewhere along
the winding route,

destruction [41]

you began to do things
you'd only heard about.

Somehow with the distance
you've invited a curse
that makes the once fun journey
feel increasingly worse.
No longer laughing
to lost now to view
the price that this homage
has required of you.

No longer enjoying
simply wanting to stop
you struggle to find a place
to rest from your walk.
Like a foot hobbled
by a stone seemingly small
you are left limping
barely moving at all.

The night is falling
you look all around,
nothing looks familiar
you strain for a sound.
An alarm or trumpet
leading you back
away from destruction
away from the pack.

Your fellow travelers
no longer look the same
their faces are deformed
by heaviness and shame.
Distorted and twisted
like shedding snake skin
you stifle the terror
bubbling within.

When did it happen?
Where was the turn?
When did this road
become a lesson learned?
How do I leave here
to get back home?
You stumble to run back
as you bite back a moan.

This was not where
you thought you'd end
when you started destruction's journey
and stepped into sin.
You stop on the pathway
that unexpectedly turned steep.
Searching the sky
as your heart weeps.
The cries of your heart
spill from your lips.
There must something
better than this.

Over the treetops
into the sky
a small light shimmers
catching your eye.
Not sure what it is
you still feel the tug.
You follow it blindly
thinking nothing of,
how long it will take
no matter how hard
your eyes stay locked,
on the shining star.

You're led to a valley
and a small clear stream.
You rest for the first time
in years it seems.
You know nothing of your location
you travel apart
for the first time in ages
following your heart.
In a moment anxious
for who can know
the directions back
to an unfractured soul.
Looking out at the road with dread
you're anxious and worried of the road ahead.
You slumber, stretched out
under a blanket of sky.

Praying the morrow's journey
won't go awry.

You wake up rested
ready to leave,
something has shifted
while you laid asleep.
Back to the place of comfort and grace.
How you got there with seemingly no trace?

A clue of your slumbered journey
from a barren land,
a single set of footsteps
lingering warmth on your hand.
All while you slumbered
someone carried you free
Asking for nothing
but a testimony.

Share of your journey
from destruction and pain.
So you will aid other travelers
in doing the same.

Statistic

I scan through the faces,
searching their eyes.
Nothing is familiar
nothing seems right.
On the corner
and racing the street.
No one is coming
to rescue me.
The men are like giants
swinging their hands.
I scream and panic,
I can't understand.
Where did my shoes go,
my purse,
my clothes?
Why did she leave me
here alone?
I search in the alleys
screaming her name
and there is a woman
doing the same.
I run out to meet her
and grasp her arms.
She is my sister,
I finally belong.

I still feel the tremors
moving under my skin.
I never want to be left
alone again.

We lock our hands
with a desperate clasp.
At least there is someone,
survival, a chance.
I thought she would come back.
I thought she would see,
that when she left this place
she forgot to take me.
I beg for some money
and see street signs
trying to remember
which path is mine.
If this is my fate
out here on the street,
I have to find shelter
and something to eat.
I stumble and hurdle
chasing the night,
I won't die here without a fight.

The Moment

No name to rely on,
I am not the natural choice.
No credentials, no pedigree
just a passionate devotion to you.

The sun has set on the fame seekers
and has begun to rise
on the lovers of your presence.

Placed in partnership with
the experienced forerunners,
I am poised to see the moment.

The moment when old becomes fresh.
When the veil between here and there is torn.

My inexperience makes me wary and fearful.
Not wanting to sully this time.

Eyes stretched and ears straining,
I am breathless in anticipation
of what may be revealed.

I glance to the old ones beside me,
trying to copy their stance.

To mirror their seeming confidence and calm.

As I fade into the background,
I see the experience at work.
Not shy or timid to enter in.

My lips part to bring in more air.
It is stifling in this moment,
the transition of them to me.

It is my moment.

Paralyzed

Standing paralyzed,
apathy has me in its' grip.
I see so much, yet care so little
numbness chokes me with its' bit.

Desensitized and uncaring
this journey has made me be,
it hurts too much to listen
to the pain that's calling me.

I hear the people crying,
the groaning and gnashing of teeth.
So I cover my ears and huddle,
so their crying voices won't reach me.

Immobile, uncaring, and unwitting
like a puppet dangling from a string.
I see so much to be done
and yet I do nothing.

But stand in my corner peering

hidden in a corners shade.
I know there must be something
for me to do to help the misery fade.

So I fill my lungs with boldness
and puff my breast upright,
I must do something, anything
I am called to fight this fight.

I step forward from my hiding place
and gaze out before
I am ready to join the battle
I am ready to do more.

Moving

Moving ever closer to your beauty
I am wooed and pulled ever still.
I will always be held by your spirit
I will always stay safe in your will.
Your Word, like a lover's letter
is held pressed close to my breast.
I have never felt anything better
than the comfort of your sweet rest.
Like dew falls slow from the morning,
your presence is hesitant to leave.
I will always stay here in your glory,
from your side I could never be.

Frayed

Frayed around the edges
depleted, tired, and worn.
Chasing after your approval
has left my heart torn.

Falling into madness
the feeling surprising and new.
I will always be left wanting
when giving myself to you.

Because your heart has seen no movement,
no blood has pumped it full.
You are a dead thing that I held to
into the void with you, I'm pulled.

I fumble to feel your pulse beat
there just beneath the skin
but, your flesh has lost all pallor
your lips have sunken in.

I stumble back aghast to know
you've been gone for quite sometime
the only heart keeping us connected
was only ever mine.

As a priest I have broken law now
forbidden to touch dead things.
I'm begging for forgiveness,
from my Savior King.

There must be something living
just beyond the veil.
Something pulsing with new promise
that leaves my past so pale.

So I stumble to the curtain
from behind it I step free.
I go running in your direction
I go running towards me.

doorway

Doorway

There's a tiny little doorway
in a tiny little hall
a small set of stairs
leads away from it all
it trails into darkness
into a basement below
the place where I seek him
the place where I go
it's here I'm stripped bare
and lay out my flesh
here I am remade,
here I'm refreshed.

Amongst the laundry
and boxes of stuff
I beg the strength
for life so rough
a chamber of prayer
my own sacred earth
a place of new focus
a place of rebirth.

Much like a man
buried in a tomb
I go here to bury
the past in this room.

Three minutes
three hours
or even three days
when I finally come up
it's like I've been raised
resurrected from all
that has gone on before
I make my way back up
to the tiny little door.

This small little doorway
is the gate I pass through
when I have no other recourse,
and I know not what to do.
Not decorated or flagrant
simple and small
my tiny little doorway
in my tiny little hall.

Battle

I don't know how it happened,
this stumbling into myself.
One moment I was lost,
the next I was found
dirty and muddy
face pressed into the ground.
I was wrong I discovered,
the feeling of success.
Doesn't feel much like celebrating,
as I brush the mud off my chest.
Because the fight has been so hard,
the war it took so long,
that winning doesn't make me
want to break out into song.
Instead I moan and whimper
my lips parched, my voice sore.
I actually made it through this time of war.

There has been so much bloodshed
some theirs, some mine.
I was not aware of all the lost time.
My victory is in my breath
still rattling below my breast.

My victory is that I haven't given up yet.
I won because I lasted
I won because I stayed
I must rest here now
another battle is on its way.

Escape

Made of stronger stuff, I am.
Held together by sheer will
and determination.
Through the course of the journey
I have remade myself.
Shaped into something stronger,
something sterner,
something made to endure.

I never knew that I had such power.
I never knew that I had such grit.
It was only for the battle
that I landed on it.

Surviving the arrows,
pulling the knives from my spine
this is how I manifested the divine.
Because as the wind buffeted me
as the storm grew strong
I dragged one foot in front of the other

and kept moving along.

I didn't know I could stand alone
until they left me.
I didn't know that I could feel joy in pain.
Until I stood on the cliff all alone
tears mixing with the rain.

I must thank them for this lesson
this gift that they taught me.
That the ability to stand alone and strong
is the true definition of being free.

I watch them writhing
in their own machinations,
obsessed and consumed with hate.
I glance my eyes to the sky and smile
I am free now,
I have escaped.

Madness

I glanced into the eyes of madness today;
I saw it swirling in her sight.
A cocktail of fear and confusion
seem sure to end in her demise.
There's something terrifying
about that look that says
I am neither here nor there.
There's something off putting
about the blankness behind her stare.
She is not with me in this moment
she is lost in a world of her own hand.
For she has fallen victim to the voices
that tell her that life must be
plotted and planned.

There is no joy there in her face,
no empathy, and no grace.
She's hardened and brutal
disgusting to behold.
This is what hatred looks like
once it has grown old.
Because she sees no value
in those she cannot use.

To be with her is like a vacuum
ever hungry to consume.
And so I back away with caution
protecting the love within.
For there is nothing more detrimental
than fighting a war you cannot win.

Love must be protected,
it cannot be tossed about.
It is my legacy,
it is my bloodline,
and to it I am devout.
I will not worship on the altar of anger,
I will not sacrifice destiny for revenge
I will not follow after madness
for down that path all good things end.

hide and seek
64

hide and seek

Not randomly chosen
I am picked to be it, the one
to search for all that's hidden.

I mask my eyes
to the plots around
I strain my ears
to catch the sound

of real locations
and true intent
tempted to spread my fingers
and peek through them.

I blow out a breath
to slow down the count
giving the players
enough time to spread out.

I am free to roam
through low hanging leaves
skirting 'round bushes
leaping roots of trees.

Skirt floating behind me
I fly o'er the ground
seemingly airborne
feet not making a sound.

When I was the hidden
I cowered in shame
now that I am chosen
I revel this game

As part of the found
my senses are keen
my eyes catching all
seen and unseen.

Not a game for children
we used to speak
a game of warfare
this hide and seek.

Greedy

I am greedy for your affection,
I am greedy for you time.
I can never settle
for less than what I feel is mine.
You said oh taste and see
and the taste still lingers on my lips.
I didn't know
that true love felt like this.
That there is no fear in this passion
not one second of remorse.
And for that I will always thank you
until my voice grows hoarse.
You will never need to look for another,
I am prepared to be your bride.
I am addicted to the voice of your heart
whispering inside.
I read your love letters,
they are solace to my soul.
Without your voice,
without your touch
I would not feel whole.
And so they ask me where to find you,
they ask me where you are.
I tell them you are everywhere

both near and far.
You have been my one true companion.
You have saved me from all things.
And for that reason my heart forever sings.
Love, oh love, how I found you,
you chased me until I caught you.
Till forever is now
and time stands on end
you are my good thing.
Amen.

Blindness

Moving ever quickly into tomorrow
I somehow missed it in today.
They have already happened,
they are here now,
the things for which I continue to pray.

I missed it in my hurry,
for it concealed itself from me.
My hopes, my very desires
aren't where I thought they'd be.

I was looking for wholeness in pits,
looking for love in the arms of rage.
I sought to find definition on someone else's page.

True love revealed itself hidden in kindness,
not parading with the mask of lust.
Happiness was hidden in service,
joy concealed itself in trust.

Like a babe discovering his toes

the answers were there all the time
the only thing that changed
was this perspective of mine.

For with new eyes I saw them
standing all about.
I'm ashamed to say I missed them
so focused on attention and clout.

Like a blind man seeking healing
it took your touch to see
that every thing I have been searching for
has already been given to me.

soul stuff

Soul Stuff

Gasping for air
I push the covers back
trying to catch the illusive thoughts.
Symptoms of a spiritual amnesiac.

Lost in a haze of stress, despondency
mind muffled and foggy
I don't remember who I'm supposed to be.

The needs of life have aborted
the desires of my heart.
The safety net I am strangling in
somehow different from the start.

This soul stuff is buried
Far beneath the skin
Trapped and unreachable
Lost far within.

The danger of life
is the mess that you make

when trying to make decisions
for safety sake.

Maybe it's better
to leap off the wall
trying to fly
risking the fall.

Regrets are mother's milk
that sustain the angst
feeding the rage
making me rail against,

anything and everyone
better than me.
That force me to remember
what I could be.

If I could just fight through the
cloudy, fear induced fog
maybe this soul stuff I would
reveal and unclog.

So I fight to be sober
not intoxicated with pain
not hobbled by apathy
and crippled by disdain.

Every once and a while
I capture a glimpse

Of the girl I once was
before the fog grew dense.

The last time I felt joy
I cannot recall
I cannot remember
when I felt anything at all.

My name I repeat
the one that they said
and yet it seems wrong
as if for someone who's dead.

The role they give me
doesn't quite fit
unless I make myself
smaller to squeeze into it.

As I press in deeper
down past my fears
around my unknowing
and cover my ears.

I can almost hear it
calling out to me
the girl I really am.
Who I'm meant to be.

It's not complete
this soul stuff work
but a start I've made
a step forward, my first.

Apologies

It's never easy to say I'm sorry.
It's difficult to apologize,
but I owe you the truth
as I stand in the mirror
looking in my own eyes.

I'm sorry that I doubted you
I'm sorry I couldn't see
how beautiful you truly are
how worthy your are, me.

I'm sorry that I abused you.
I'm sorry I let you fall.
I'm sorry I let you hide
behind that towering wall.

I'm sorry I let you worry.
I'm sorry I let you stand in fear.

I'm sorry that you felt so lost
for so many years.

I'm sorry I let you search
without ever finding the cure.
I'm sorry I didn't show you
how high you could truly soar.

I'm sorry I didn't speak louder
I'm sorry I let you hear
all the negativity around you,
when I was so near.

There is no excuse for how I failed you
I did it, I apologize.
My only consolation
is the promise
that I will never again compromise.

I will fight for you harder.
I will stand in the gap.
I will never let you fall
so far into the deceivers trap.

I will risk myself to see you.
I will hear you when you call.
I'm sorry that you had to feel
so alone through it all.

Shadows

Like a shadow looming behind you
she is always there.

Whispering sweet nothings
against the lobe of your ear.

I see that she controls you
she is hooked inside your mind.

She has muted all that's beautiful
there's nothing left behind.

The seeds she's planted of discord
are starting to take bloom.

They are watered with her lies
the truth is left no room.

For she profits from your madness

she gains from your disgrace,
through lies and whispers of evil
she has moved you from your place.

The place where peace has freedom
to twirl and move about.

You are drowning in the poison
that seeps from out her mouth.

I can cry no longer
for the girl you used to be.

For somewhere between then and now
a decision was made of thee.

To lull about in anger
to swim the waves of rage.

My only prayer for you
is left upon this page.

I pray that grace somehow finds you
that you hearken when Mercy calls your name.

That when offered a chance for loveliness
you do not reject her, once again.

I pray that your voice returns
and that you find a chance to be

the girl with the bracketed smile
who used to smile at me.

Betrayer

They are hands that I held
eyes in which I've gazed
ears that I've spoken in
smiles that I've craved.

Arms that I held to
shoulders I've clutched
a heart that I sought out
when life seemed tough.

I stand bound and restrained
in the public square.
Put there by a comrade
a friend for whom I cared.

Not cared in the past,
for I somehow care now
for my betrayer
who ordered my final bow.

The kiss was expected
revealed during sleep
no less difficult
the carnage prepared for me.

There are no words imagined
that can possibly explain
the betrayal of friendship
bringing such pain.

I see her face
in the jeering crowd
hearing her voice
as she screams out loud,
"hang her, destroy her, do it now"
my heart is broken,
my head is bowed.

Despite what I've been through
and it's been quite a lot
nothing hurts worse
than a friend's revealed plot.

Trust so hard gained

to her I gave it free
maybe I deserve to hang
for loving blindly.

if my legs weren't tied
I'd run through the throng
of people she's joined
to condemn me of wrong.

Yes, things changed
I accepted the cross
I couldn't resist
the love that it brought.

It meant that our friendship
had to shift
the things we once did
I could no longer fit.

I admit I changed
a person new,
one thing remained
my love for you.

A slight change in her affect
a twist in her lips
my new life's salvation
led us to this.

The pain of the execution

lessens in compare
to the gutted feel
of a once loved betrayer.

Our former kinship
provides her knives
that cut me in places
only known by sharing lives.

As the sun halos my head
I look at her laughing
our friendship dead.

I think of what I've lost
and whom I have gained
and to say I know him
I'd do it again.

For with her rejection
I fell on my face
I sought his guidance
I begged his grace.

The plot may hold me
but I am not bound,
for where I lost friendship
forever love I found.

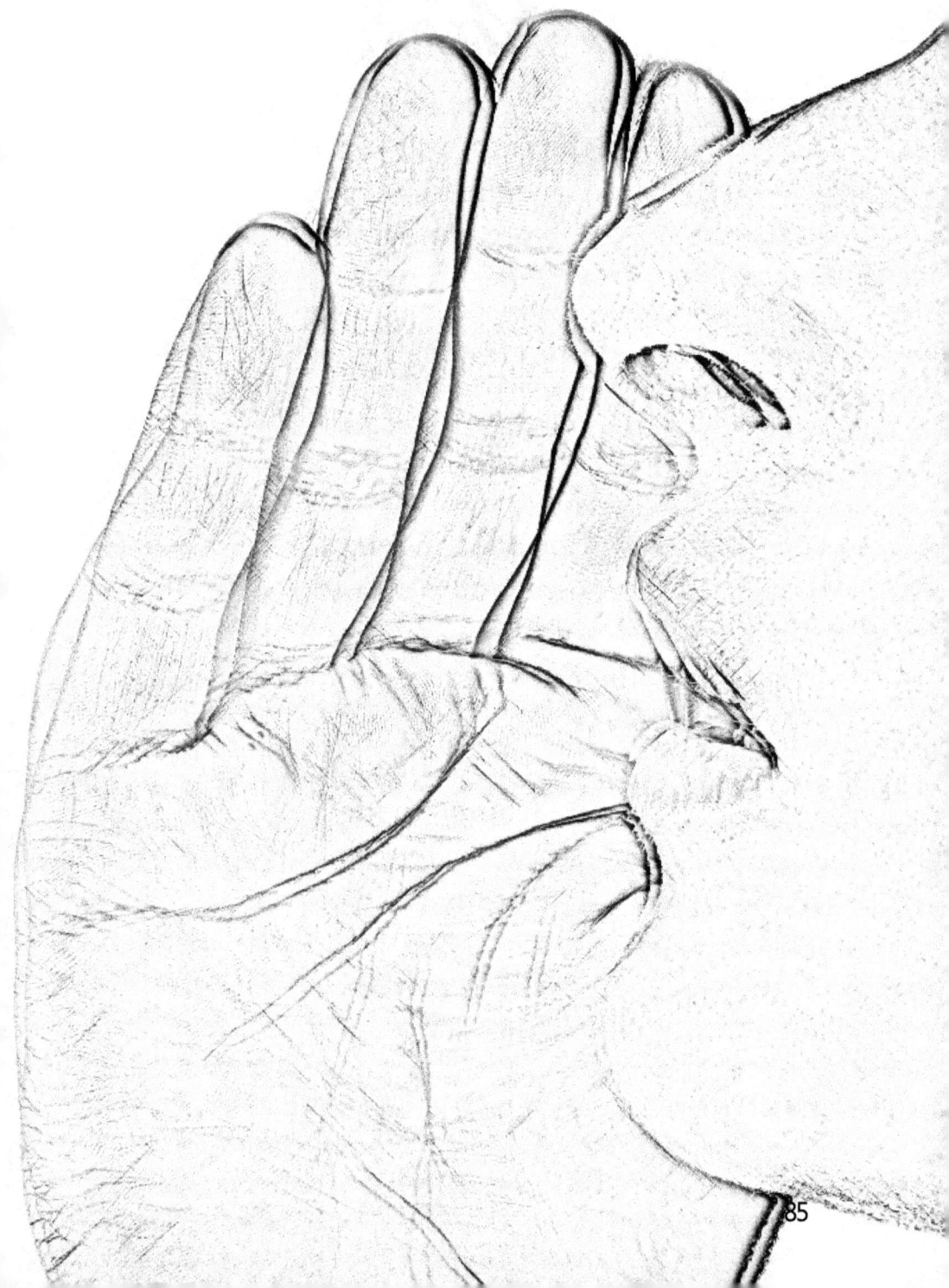

shhhh.....

shhhh...

Like a game of telephone
the word was passed
from tongue tip to eardrum
spreading fast.

The gossip of a family
causing unrest.
Whose son was a maverick
creating a mess.

Speaking in temples
spreading a word
of a new revelation
the repercussions unheard.

Rumors of dead men
leaping to life
stories of teachings
causing divide.

Who is this rebel
causing dissent?
How can we remove his
growing regiment?

His powerful presence
creating a stir
making it difficult
for tradition to be preserved.

Many years later
looking at you,
the rumors still linger
the presence still true.

For now you carry
the secret thing
that changed humanity
that birthed a King.

You wonder why your taunted,
tracked, and pursued?
The treasure was buried
deep inside you.

Withstand all the whispers
important they are not
you can't control it,
it will never stop.

Though you may not see it
the world is not blind
the secret you carry

is the divine.

A hush settles
when you walk in the room
for they recognize
who lives in you.

The secret is spreading
no longer concealed
the time is coming
the time to reveal.

All that is hidden
will be brought to life
and the secret remnant
will arise.

Deception

I cannot deny that you once enticed me
I cannot deny you held appeal,
you were deceiving in your nature
for your kindness seemed so real.

You wooed me with your laughter.
You seduced me with your smile.
You plotted my demise
holding hands with me all the while.

I am angry, I am enraged
but not with you, you see.
I am angry that I believed you
I am angry with me.

For I should have known better.
I should have been more wise.
I should have known that as the debtor
I would have to pay the price.

For where you once gave,
you now demanded.

From where you once sowed, you took.
You plotted and bartered my slavery
and you invited others to look.

I dangled there as a testament
that naiveté is a sin.
I am angry that if I had the chance
I would fall prey to you once again.

Abba

In a world of prepackaged everything
I sometimes find it hard to define
all that you were, are, and will be
this father of mine.

Like a kid playing dress up
I try to walk in your imprint
but, it forever swallows me up
your greatness I can't seem to fit.

Your unmatched presence
overwhelms my life so small.
I am always stunned
that you love me at all.

The family name I've battered
with shame, guilt, and sin.
I stink of the pigs I've played with
the filth I've wallowed in.

Beneath the filth you see me,
beyond the pigpen you call.
You run out to meet me
not repulsed at all.

It is that, I can't explain to them,
the ones who ask me why.
When I think of your freely given love
I softly begin to cry.

There has never been another
who knows me through and through.
Therefore, there could never be another
who loves me quite like you.

Naked, on display, is my shame
and yet you still call me by name.
Not the labels they have hurled at me
by strangers who know me not
but, the loving name of daughter
a name that cannot be bought.

It cannot be packaged and bartered
like an ordinary thing.
It can only be gifted
by the one who makes my heart sing.

My one, my only
my Abba father, I call.

Thank you for seeing me
for loving me at all.

the tarnished pulpit

The Tarnished Pulpit

Worn down by use
it stands with a slight sway
listing ever so to the left
once shining with new intent
the years have dampened the sheen
the sides bear the imprint
of hands clenched with life to convey
sweat drops rain down marring the surface
and yet there has been no perspicacity
no new discernment to unveil
shrouded now in fodder and pretensions
robbed of its' beauty for lack of devotion
once an altar of purpose
now a marker of what once existed
mourners once praisers
come to visit the place where he was
searching violently to find where he is now
once found we will visit no longer
to this monument of the past
pressing forward to the promises of new wine.

Dreamer

Disconnected from the world
I slumber
tucked safely away in bed.
It is here that I see him
appearing in my head.
With his creator hand he paints for me,
world's seen and not yet seen.
It is here that he speaks to me
truth and the deeper things.
I see myself lift up
he takes me by the hand.
He pulls from this world to his
and he speaks as only he can.
I hear his voice,
though his lips do not move.
Heart to heart
and soul to soul
is how we commune.
I'm addicted to his presence
I beg him, "let me stay,
let me linger in your beauty
each and every day."

His hand on my shoulder
his breath blowing through my heart
I settle back into myself
a new morning to start.
His loveliness it lingers
on the palate like new wine.
He is my soul's lover
forever mine.

Victory

Blinking the sweat from my eyes
I stop winded and look about.
The field is scattered
dead soldiers surround.

Longer than I expected
this battle reigned on,
so many years spent here
so much time gone.

I fall to my knees
fist pressed to my breast.
I am shocked that I lasted
through this last test.

Head swiveling about
eyes lolling round in my head.
My body throbbing,

my arms heavy
my armor stained blood red.

When I was sitting on the sidelines
I thought I understood
what it meant to be a member
a solider tried and good.

But when you are left alone
knees digging in the sand
tears mixing with sweat and blood
you finally understand.

The hardest part of battle
comes right at the end
when you look around you
and see so few friends.

You knew there would be loss
that little would remain
but shocked you are to find
how much you would gain.

For the few that lasted
the handful you have still
this is the battle treasure
for this you were almost killed.

Not the gold or the silver
but the word on your lips

the war story of your victory
your true battle prize, is this.

Calling

I hear the ticking of time
it beckons and calls my name.
I hear my pulse racing
begging release from the mundane.
I am propelled out into the open
by the force of my own call.
I didn't ask for this mantle
not, once, not at all.
While I was praying to be relevant
I was asking to be tried.
When I begged to be effective
with opposition, heaven replied.
In searching for wisdom
I kept finding war.
In seeking prosperity
I was told to give more.
Had I known what I was asking
would I have done the same?
Yes, I must answer
for the glory of His name.

Lovelorn

I have loved and lost
and through it all
the truth remains the same.

I would have rather loved
than not at all
to me this would be a shame.

To miss the chance to soar so high
that life seems
naught but a dream.

To feel so full and so complete
that I could do anything.

My one regret is wasted time
the time we spent apart.

I held you back
away and at bay
trying to protect my heart.

Somehow bravery won

and we took the chance,
the chance to begin anew.

I never thought
I could be in love
until the day I loved you.

passionate love

Passionate Love

Lascivious and unending is his love for me

overwhelmingly present

pulsing right above the skin

there is nothing more powerful

than to tap into that kind of love

that moves freely

between forever and this moment

quickening everything that it touches

this kind of love brings new life

to the dead things it connects with

resurrecting new dreams and promises

bringing life back to dead hearts

and buried dreams

there is something so beautiful

and yet so graphic about this kind of love

not the stuff of fairy tales and store-bought cards

it is a bloody, gory, stretched high type of love

one that is calling out to be reciprocated daily

I am ever humbled by its completeness

I am moved beyond comprehension

there is no similitude to its passion

the fullness of it is more than can fit in the mind,

the heart and the soul

in moments I access pieces of it

intimidated to swallow it whole

once touched you race back again and again

with an incessant need

it is bold in its behavior

and mocks all that attempts to replicate it,

it walks in pageantry and simplicity

it is all things big

I'm amazed that it exists

who can describe it

so many have tried

there is no combination of words and phrases

commas and periods

seems redundant to list all that it is

like a newborn colt

I am stumbling over myself to access it

more than anything I've ever dreamed

I am consumed by it

for someone who was so lost

it has been an awakening for me

like an infant stretching its eyes after slumber

I am taken aback by the largeness of it all

hovering over me

wrapped around me

rubbed into me

the fragrance lingers on the skin

I am hesitant to point out all the ways

in which this love is wasted on someone like me

unworthy, true

unrecognized, of course

and yet loved passionately

I cannot explain.

Safe

With no strain
and no force
You held back the sun.

Through the power of your love
my night was undone.

With the breath of your will
the strength of your might
you gave me more time
to get it right.

Unseen, I slipped through peril.

Untouched, I escaped death.

With no scent of smoke
in hell I found rest.

Exhausted and ashamed
you heard as I called you
whispering your name.

Knees shaking and limbs weak,

you came to see me
I heard you speak.

My heart knew your voice
before my eyes could look.

Tears leaking from the corners
like a small steady brook.

Like fresh wind
from the Mount of Hermon
new life cocooned me
from all sides

Thank you my soul's lover
for saving my life.

Rapidly

Moving rapidly
through time and space
my fear is that I'll be left behind.

The panic grips
the paranoia mounts
as I look for directional signs.

Signs that point me
towards my destiny.

Signs that make the path seem clear.
When you're lacking in direction
everything seems far from here.

I used to be able,
to see my competitors,
we ran along the same track.

But somewhere through the years
I separated from the pack.

Though painful the separation
through time it became clear.
That the tearing away was necessary
for me to truly hear.

The call was not for many
the task was just for me.
The sacrifice for attaining glory
was to live completely free.

Of those who could not journey
for this path is steep and hard.
I remain focused on the calling
keeping it tucked against my heart.

I no longer hear the footsteps.
I no longer hear the cries.
It is silent along this path.
This journey of mine.

Standstill

It is slippery,
this place of in between,
not stable,
so unsure.
Having no foundation to rest on
makes you susceptible
to the lure.
Voices that make you promises,
that swear to bring you bliss.
There is much danger in Judas' kiss.
Knowing not who you are
and what you believe.
Makes you bait for the captor
and easy to deceive.
One mind, two masters
is unsteady like the shore.
Ever pulled into the ocean
returning no more.

There is safety in standing

there is victory in not being moved.
Standstill and be confident
don't let them pursue.
Defend the ground you fought for.
It is yours freely with no mar or blight,
to stake your claim in history
as the owner with dominion rights.
No one can shake you
unless you let them near.
Standstill and have courage
never bow down in fear.

fishermen

Fishermen

You must be using
the wrong bait
here on this boat.
Been fishin' for days
without any hope.
Not one catch
not one changed soul,
you're supposed to be a fisherman
but fishin' gets old,
when you stand on the water
seeing nothing but blue
and the responsibility
for bringing in fish
rests on you.
You thought if you stood here
and cast out your rod
you'd easily win souls for God.
Could be that what you're using
seems not to take
because fish want real food
not happy with fake.
You cast out the perception
of everything right
fish aren't looking at the bait

they're watching your life.
Do you show that being captured
is the desired place to be?
That being bound in salvation
is better than being free.
So you can stand in the water
for years and years
never making a dent
never bringing in new hearers.
Called to be fishermen
catchers of men?
I think you need to bait your hook again.
This time using your testimony
throw out your life
showing the benefit
of being with Christ.
I know that you been fishin'
toiling all night.
Go ahead and cast your net
this time on the right.
Be transparent in your discipleship
bare it all
the cost of being a fisher of men
and answering the call.

More

I cling to the hope
that there is something out there.

Something larger than myself.

I pray that there is something bigger
a greater story to tell.

I'm desperate to see more,
to push the limits of every new day.

I want to never run out of
beautiful things to say.

More laughter.
More passion.
More joy,
and more grace.

I want to never slow down the pace.

To forever keep chasing after all that is good.

To never settle for could, should,
or would.

To press in deeper.
To surrender more.
To empty out everything
till the last pour.

To bask in sunlight,
until the sky turns gray.

To never waste a moment,
to never lose my way.

Covenant

We cannot shout here
we cannot make one sound.
We have entered into the sacred,
we stand on holy ground.

For this is the place of promise
the place where covenant is made.
The place where fresh skin is cut by the blade.

This moment requires sacrifice
a burnt offering to give.
It is covenant that something must die
in order for something to live.

We will mark this ground with an altar,
a monument to this day.
So the story of the sacrifice
will never fade away.

Slicing the thickness of silence
I hear whistling at the top of the trees.
It is there that the message
comes raining down to me.

The truth of his promise
pierces through the skin,
I am filled with new glory pulsing from within.

I have to be quiet
in order to hear
the time is now coming,
yea the time is near.

I pause crouched in the thicket
the bushes act as a shroud.
I lick my lips and point my ear to the clouds.

I look like a madman
lips murmuring to the sky.
I ask for permission to pursue
then let out a battle cry.

My feet slap against the wet earth
hardly making a sound,
I am all alone on this field
there's nothing around.

The war is in the mind's eye,
the hardest fight to win
is not the one with foes around
but the one waging deep within.

This enemy is cunning.
Her sword it swings without haste

I stumble as I try to block out,
this enemy shares my face.

The greatest battle I have ever fought
was the one I fought with me.
Wrestling with the inner man
is a bittersweet type of victory.

For with winning
comes great relief,
I am somehow free.
I rest in the knowledge
that once again, I have conquered me.

the masses

The Masses

I am not one of the masses
different and somehow strange
not cut from the same cloth
not a child of rage;

I cannot follow the lost ones
who act without thought
never one to settle
for being traded and bought;

I am more than this title
more than this place
more than the money
you wave in my face;

I'll never bow down
I'll never give in
just like Daniel
I will always defend;

the name that is lifted

the name that has saved
the one who keeps me
the one who paid;

the price for my name change
paid off the debt
allowed to live freely
not beholden to death;

I can't ignore
when the false speaks bold
like a little boy on the sidelines
who to a giant told;

you cannot speak against
the almighty one
you uncircumcised Philistine
the battle has begun;

I cannot stare blindly
as evil prevails
till my last breathe
I will fight against hell;

defending the chosen
the remnant that remains
is not for the masses
just for the saved.

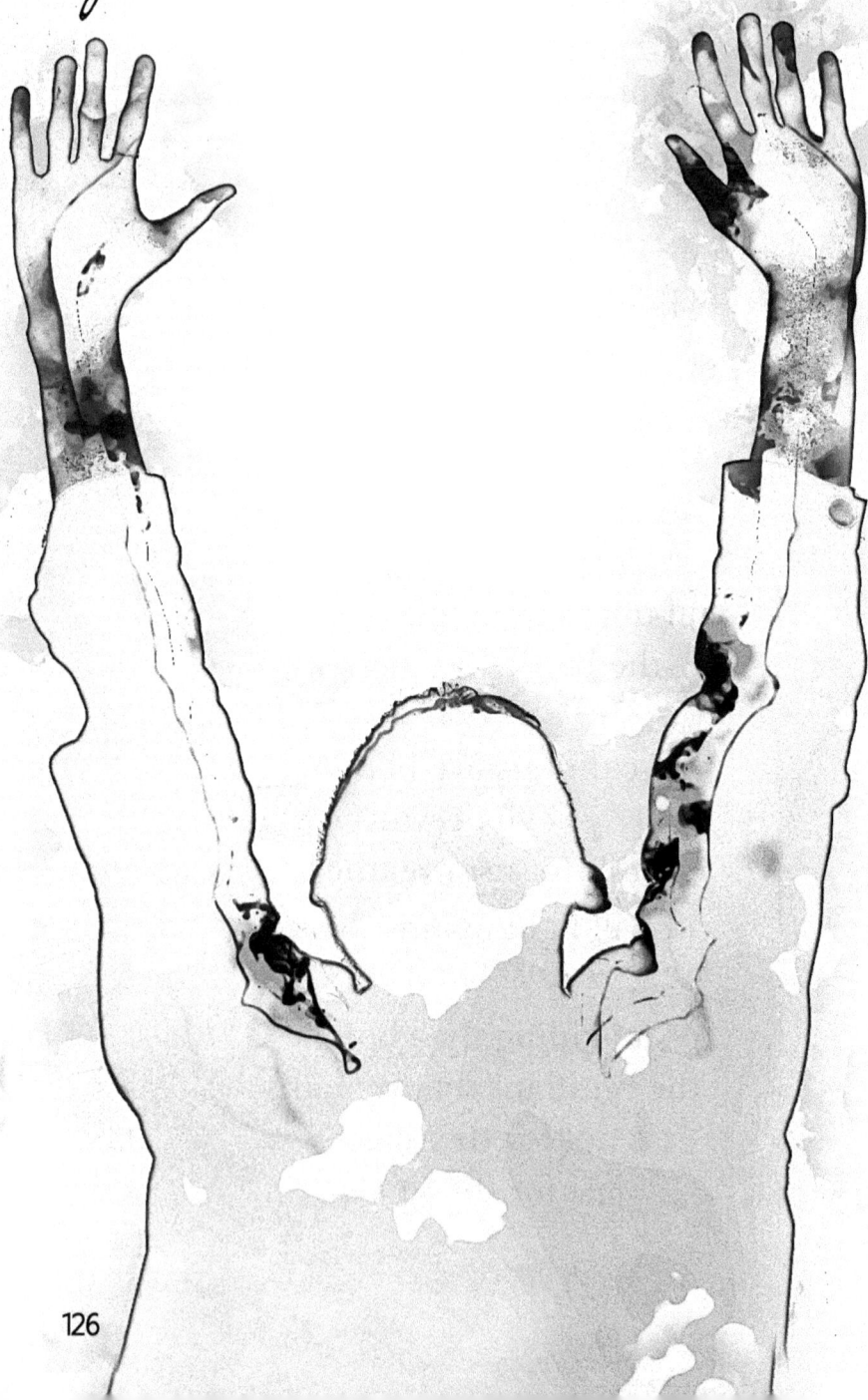

protector

Protector

Who can rescue me when I'm dying
Who will answer when I call
Who will chase away the demons
Who threaten to take it all;

Who will help me when I'm broken
Who will see me through this mess
Who will keep me from destruction
Who will help me pass this test;

Who will defend me from the liar
Who will cover me from the plots
Who will perch me standing upright
Who will cleanse my damaged thoughts;

Who will never leave me defenseless
Who will always take away pain
Who will advocate when I'm silenced
Who will guide me through the rain;

Who will give me sweet respite
Who will calm my weeping heart
Who will cause me to have joy
Who will never stay afar;

Who will call a thousand angels
Who will destroy an opposer's regime
Who will wipe them out from near me
Never to be seen again;

Who is the one who promised
Who was the one who led
Who is the one shining
love down over my head;

Who can tell me secrets
that change my very soul
Who can lead me to Rehoboth
With no price or toil;

Who loves me completely, madly
Who fills me fresh each day
Who makes me better
Who shows me the way;

Who tells me I'm valued
Who gave me a name
Who holds me closely
and invites me the same;

Who is this father
that loves me so
embracing his daughter
never letting go.

Maybe

Maybe this time will be different,
maybe I won't slip so far.

Maybe this time I'll manage
to find where you are.

Maybe you won't see me
when I slip into the dark.

Maybe you will leave me
if I don't play the part.

Of a girl whose heart is happy,

with no bruises or cares.

That is mighty to stand
and not afraid or scared.

Maybe beneath the bravado
is a timid little girl.

Who wants more than anything
to have you in her world.

Who doesn't know the rituals
or the proper protocol.

Who isn't really interested
in fitting in at all.

Like an unrefined fisherman
with a temper and a blade.

Maybe I tend to act first
and then listen to what you say.

Maybe I could be used of you?

Maybe there is a plan,
not based on the opinions of man.

Maybe beneath the indifference
you can see how much I care.

Maybe you can see in me
something precious and rare.

Maybe you'll see past the part of me,
wet behind the ears.

Maybe you have been with me
for, oh so many, years.

Maybe I can be better than
the hypocrisy I see.

Maybe I am worthy
of you loving me.

Comfortable

My eyes are open
yet all I see is black.

The space is tight pressed
against me front and back.

I've been down here for quite some time.
Burrowed deep in this little pit of mine.

I hate that it holds me
away from the sun.

I'm soothed by it's comfort
for I know nothing else but.

This tiny little place
in this black confined hole.

This tiny black pit
hidden in my soul.

When I first fell in it
I would scream and shout,

wanting nothing more
than to be let out.

I'd cry until my voice grew hoarse
screaming, "Someone, pull me out, please."

I screamed until spittle formed
around my mouth, visible to see.

I heard a voice whisper back
hovering over me,

promising me escape
saying I could be free.

In exchange for this rescue
I was asked just one thing,

to leave the pit and not return
and bring with me nothing.

I paused in silence
this is hard to say;

I hate my pit and I love it
I fear I always may.

Yes, it confines me
keeping me from love.

But it's scary outside the pit
the world up above.

Here in this blackness
there is no demand,

asking me to be better
asking me to expand.

Like a fish without water
I fear I couldn't breathe,

if I couldn't keep a small part
of my little pit with me.

I'm sorry, that I asked for help
that I asked to be free.

I think I didn't realize
how hard it would truly be.

So leave me in this pit of mine
so restricted yet so secure.

I'm not ready to be free yet.
I'm not ready for more.

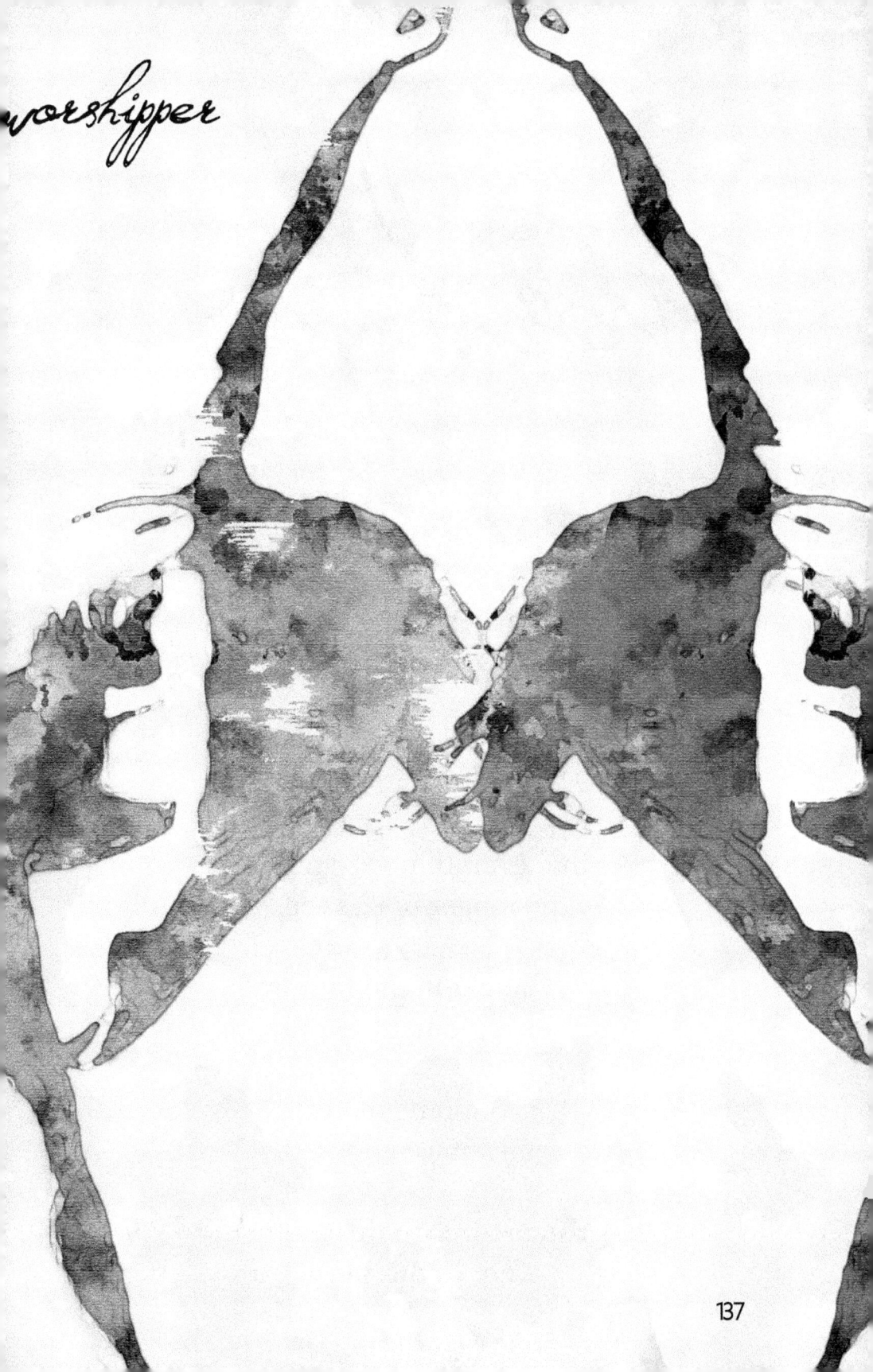

worshipper

Worshipper

I can see how David
danced right out of his clothes.

Moving with abandon
trapped in the throes,

of a moment of worship
so pure and intense,

that everything around you
no longer makes sense.

Caught in the rapture
of a moment so pure.

Slipping out of
all you've endured.

You are free in this moment
not in this place,

but up amongst heavens
and seeing his face.

It is here I find healing
and joy to spare.

There can be no substitute
able to compare.

Bystanders may look on us in shock,
judging how out of control we look.

The price we pay
they can never truly know.

The cost of worship
is pain that doesn't show.

We dance because we're broken.
We laugh because we've cried.

We leap as a testament
to being freed from the ties.

A life of crucifixion
for we die each day.

These moments of worship
enable us to say,

that we praise him in the morning,
the breaking of the sun.

We praise him
at midnight when the day is done.

We worship through song, lyre, and dance.
We'd stay in this moment forever, given the chance.

The worship seeps
from the cracks in my life.

The place where the potter
has shaped with the knife.

The bruising and forming causes pain
for this reason I praise his name.

Eyes closed, heart opened up
I will praise him forever
with my worship.

Conversion

~First~

I can't really tell you
what it feels like to be new.

I don't feel all together different
unsure what to do.

I said it and I meant it,
I'm ready for a change.

What that really means for me
I just can't explain.

I know I can't go back
to where I used to be.

I don't yet know where I'm going
or what is meant for me.

I'm certain that I have so much
pain buried down inside.

And I know that nothing else has worked
from the many things I've tried.

I didn't find it in the arms of men
or snorted up my nose.

I didn't find it in
the cuts I hide buried beneath my clothes.

Empty did it leave me
the money that I've made.

Happiness and peacefulness
I couldn't purchase or pay.

~Second~

I can't really tell you
what it feels like to be new.

Trying to explain a big God
and all that he can do.

I know you don't feel different
unsteady in your ways.

But your heart responded when you heard him
which means you've already begun to change.

Your right, there is nothing
left for you out there.

No person, no drug, no thing, no place
can make the pain easier to bear.

Your purpose, you will find it
revealed in his plan.

No one can heal your heart,
quite like he can.

I've been there, I get it
that pain that you spoke of.

I've seen it and I've lived it
before I found his love.

It all left me empty
the alcohol, the drugs, and clothes.

It would have never filled me,
how could I have known.

Till I stumbled to the altar
and fell to me knees.

Until I surrendered
every broken part of me.

~First~

I'm scared that I won't be happy.
I'm scared that I'm not changed.

I'm scared that when I wake up
I'll still feel pain.

I'm scared I can't live up to
what I should be.

I'm scared that salvation works
for everyone but me.

I'm scared that I'll slip back
into addiction and shame.

I'm scared that I'll wish for
death all over again.

I'm scared that I'm not like
the good people that I see.

I guess, what I'm saying is
I'm scared that I'm not worthy.

Of his sacrifice and his patience
of his protection and his love.

Do you think that he can fix me

from all I'm broken of?

~Second~

You'll be more than happy,
instead having peace and joy.

You'll be more than changed
because you have been reborn.

The truth is you will feel pain
you can't escape it in this life.

The good news is that it will only visit
never staying past it's time.

Salvation isn't mathematics
a formula to be solved.

It's a love letter to your broken heart
written before the world revolved.

Fear is your enemy
it will try to chase you down.

It will try to suffocate you
so his voice cannot be found.

You fear you're not worthy?
The opposite is true,

the reason there is salvation at all
is because of you.

For you he suffered.
For you died.

For you he was resurrected,
you are the reason why.

You will never fully know
the depth of his matchless love for you.

So instead of trying to explain it
just love him for making you new.

Daddy

I could hear the whistling
long before I saw the steam.
The pressure of his daily life
made him vicious and mean.
Trapped with a madman
who screams and shouts
that was the childhood,
of which I wanted out.

I knew that he loved me
and hated me the same.
The strategy of avoiding him
became the family game.

In clergy wear dressed pious
we perfected the act,
of the perfect Christian family
happy and intact.

But the facade was exhausting,

he couldn't keep the mask.
Pretending that he cared for us
a burdensome act.

His arms grew tired
of punches and hits.
His feet grew weary
of chasing and kicks.

The women,
the money,
the title,
the name.
This was his altar,
the place where he came.

He had no scent of holiness.
His speech no trace of God.
His disguise no longer concealing
all he was guilty of.

A final indiscretion
one too many times.
This time when he walked away
no connections left to bind.

He drifted away
like a leaf in the wind.
It would be years

before we'd see him again.

Still dressed for the pulpit
still playing the game.
This time with new players
with slightly different names.

He found the new actors
who would dance all around,
but the secrets of his
tendencies still floated about.

Still hitting,
still kicking,
still ugly
and disturbed.

New family,
same madman
nothing new learned.

Age is now his abuser
he cannot make amends.
He is robbed of time to get it right
before his life here ends.

What happens to a madman
who's losing his prime?
Where does the anger go
when it stays trapped in his mind?

No outlet to vent it,
no strength left to fight.
It may look like a change
or maybe it might,

be that the body is aging
so he sits and he stews.
Fixated on the lost ones
the family of his youth.

I can't say that I know him
this stranger to me.
My prayer is that salvation
shifts his identity.

From trickster to kinsmen,
from unknown to named.
His gift to us was leaving
taking with him the pain.

Regret is now his namesake
the true heir to his tarnished throne.
I'm thankful for the absence
for leaving us alone.

For where he left a void
true love came and filled the gap.
The beauty of redemption
is getting abundance back.

For the years of pain we suffered
we have been rewarded with more.
More security and peacefulness
overflowing what we asked for.

What happens when a madman
finally says goodbye?
You finally start living.
You finally have life.

noose

Noose

I can feel it tightening
the noose around my neck.
Tighter than I remember
my hands grappling to check.
I feel oxygen blocked
between my lungs and my brain.
This is the feeling of going insane.

I wish that this noose
was twine and rope.
Instead I am hanged
by a lack of hope.
Without its presence
I have no chance to be,
a shining example
of your faith in me.

So mired in dogma
and appropriateness,
that there is no room
for God to bless.

Pharisees suffocate me
they condemn me with law.
I am stoned by unbelievers
who doubt your call.
Betrayal and deception
flooding out the pews.
So much carnality,
so little you.

Where can I find you
but tucked in your word.
How can I answer
if your voice isn't heard.
My body is flailing
at the end of this rope.
My body is dying
being cut off from hope.

Though many sing
and many shout
the tone is empty
and hollowed out.
More churches than casinos.
One on each block.
Why then, so ineffective
glory sealed and locked?

Despite the numbers
that report to be.

I see so few believers
who will stand with me.
For this cause, we should
be willing at least;
to feed the hungry
and wash their feet.
To comfort the widow
and parent the lost.
To share in their burdens
to show them the cross.

Yet we ourselves are mourning,
still outside the grave.
We can't share the resurrection
still standing by the cave.
Waiting for a sign
that the Savior has raised.
That death no longer has us
trapped and afraid.

Somehow we missed it,
seduced by an amnesiac fog.
We forgot the simple meaning
of this, our commissioned call.

We've used it to belittle
to stifle and judge.
Those whose sin is different
than the ones we're guilty of.

We head to the building
thinking it's the church.
Forgetting where ministry
is truly birthed.

Not in a building of concrete
or one of steel
but down in our bellies
where the truth reveals,
the map of his purposes
the shape of his plan.
I'm afraid that our altars
are worshipping man.

So that's why you stand there
impotent of change.
This is why the new wine
has passed you again.
For while you sit in judgment
of the world you deem so small.
God is using new voices
that don't look like you at all.

They're young and tattooed.
Rumpled and unrefined.
These will be the chosen
to usher in the divine.
Their only care is truthfulness,
not titles,
not fame.

Just the all together power
of the Savior's beautiful name.

These will be the ones
bringing back wonders and signs.
They will be the ones
plucked fresh from the vine.

For they lived through your hypocrisy
and saw enough to know.
Sometimes the greatest enemies of tomorrow
are ones who saw yesterday go.

The Winding Road

This winding road
has traveled me far
lifted me up
broken my heart.

I am changed in the journey
transformed in the walk.
The pace is confused
an inconsistent stop and start.

Scattered spurts of progress
make measurement moot.
Destination looming
overshadowing each foot.

The path is bitter
though beautifully landscaped
ever pushing me upward
allowing me to chase,

after all that I see
lurking in my sleep
just beyond consciousness
just out of reach.

the winding road

I run when I'm able
I walk when I'm in pain
I hobble when I'm broken
I crawl across rough terrain.

The path of this life
has promised to be
more myrrh than sweetness
a bitter cup for me.

The cloud of your glory
covers me complete.
Your wind cools my tears
your grace guides my feet.

A weary traveler
on an unpaved road
no directional markers
to guide me home.

Just the urging of promise
beating in my chest
offering comfort
promising rest.

The road it slopes
taking me low
the sun out of eyesight
the temperature cold.

This part of the road
is not for the young
only interested in serving
God in the sun.

This is for the travelers
who've traveled some time
who know that the Father
also covers the night.

The mystery of this road
comes in the bends
that come without warning
moving you in

to new stretches of land
not in your plan
taking you places
no one else can.

A place of new insight
and wonderful growth
where freedom is offered
with no reproach.

The one consistent hazard
of traveling this road
is that most of your travels
will be done alone.

Part of the process
is learning to move
when everything is challenged
and you see nothing new.

No new road of purpose
no second chance
no side road to bypass
the pit in your path.

Required to leap
when barely you stand
told to have faith
when you don't think you can.

Spectators stand
on the side of the road
watching you struggle
offering taunts to goad.

More like an arena
on one side a lair
a lion pacing restless
seeking his fare.

Though solely you've traveled
mostly unseen
part of the road
is public indeed.

Eager to judge you
to see how you fall
when nothing is around you
to protect you at all.

Your mind flies swiftly
back through this path
and reminders of pitfalls
over which you have passed.

Buoyed by remembering
you take a brave leap
hands lifted high
air under your feet.

You up and jump
into the arms of your love
eyes closed and trusting
the help from above.

You land on the other
side of the test
a praise on your lips
a song in your breast.

So thankful for surviving
you never look back
to see if the spectators
offer a hand clap.

Wiping the dirt
from your bending knees
you again start moving
still traveling.

This winding road
on this long hard path
the sun in your face
your back to the past.

Underwater

Like a man lying on the ocean
I exhale and sink deep
surrendering to the water
as it washes over me.

This is baptism
the surrendering to more
the purification of humanity.
First Savior, now Lord

Deception is easy
in the game of giving in
you think wrongly by standing
that you always win.

Sometimes victory comes
when you fall to your knees
and surrender to his grace
and to his mercy.

Curls springing with water

creeping up past my ears
covering my face
blending with tears.

The submerging of the old man
the dying away of flesh
leaves me broken and open
to welcome the next.

My eyes closed underwater
and yet I see clear
the course of my life like a flipbook
year after year.

I see where he shadowed me
when I didn't even know.
I see where he covered me
everywhere I'd go.

I'm ashamed to admit
all that he's seen me do
and yet I'm free because
he knows me through and through.

Despite what I've survived
and despite what he's seen
this moment is ours
by the edge of the sea.

No chance to feel like drowning

in a moment my body presses through
forced to the surface
shaking and new.

Eyes clapping themselves open
looking at the shore
other broken children
ready for more.

The power of this moment
is the complete lack of time
for a split-second underwater
you access the divine.

At once entered into heaven
time standstill
and you bask in the glory
of being in his will.

I can feel how much he loves me.
I can feel that he's so proud
that I'm ready to carry the gospel
and proclaim his name out loud.

Eyes wet more from weeping
and less of the sea.
The confusion of feeling different
and knowing the old me.

Like a split screen in the mind

I am caught in between
old man and new man
but peacefully serene.

So definitively changed
I walk murmuring his praise.
I could stay in this moment
until the end of days.

Tomorrow

The first step was difficult,
the second not so hard.
The third step less timid,
soon I was racing through the yard.

Slamming out the gate,
next flying over the field
creating distance behind me,
chasing the surreal.

I stop on the edge of an orchard
my back against a tree.
I lift my eyes over my shoulder
to see what awaits for me.

My eyes swing back to look
at the place from which I've come.
I feel no sense of connection
I am finished there,
I'm done.

My breath has been restored
I brace my palms against the bark
I launch myself like a ship
running forward, chasing my heart.

My lungs continue to bellow
pushing in and out
air coursing through my body
I let slip a joyful shout.

Illusively out there,
like a phantom's dream.
It seemed just a fantasy
this future set before me.

Hope stands there in the future
calling back to me
guiding me ever forward
helping me to believe.

Encouraging me to move
telling me to make haste
there is more for me to do
my life I cannot waste.

I stumble in my excitement
and yet I do not stop
the day turns to evening
resting is not a thought.

As night folds over into day
and God places the moon in the sky
I am desperate to keep moving forward
I cannot explain why.

I just know that time is slipping
and for the first time, it seems in years
the momentum inside of me is building,
my days more laughter than tears.

I'm awakened from the minutia
I've been released from the mundane
the time to build has come
I can no longer play.

Tomorrow is awaiting me
the responsibility is mine
I will not be accused of the sin
of wasting given time.

The destination of tomorrow
is not just for me
but for the others yet to come
the runners yet to be.

Stretching

Moving rapidly between forever and now
is a moment
as thick as fresh-baked bread
ripe with the possibility
to do more, to say more, to become more.
I am hesitant to enter in
the infinite tension between what is
and what could be
calls out to the creator DNA that resides in me.
There is something about emptiness
that beckons me to create.
I am a seed planted, dormant
crushed beneath the weight of life
the husk of me dying under the pressure.
Yet inside of me something new and fresh begs to
emerge.
I push my way through the suffocation of that which
attempts to bury me.
As I peek out of darkness I am surprised at how

large the opportunity is.
I feel so small and yet everything within me cries out
to climb higher and taller, thicker and more sturdy.
It is impossible to resist the call
there is more to be done and
so I continue to press upward toward my creator.
Stretching up on my tippy toes
like the first day of ballet class
unsteady in my foundation
yet determined to stretch taller
as I lift my face on high.
I am moved beyond comprehension
for there between the clouds and the sky
beyond the sun and the moon
hovering somewhere over the stars
I can sense him staring back at me
with love so overwhelming I am tempted to shrink
back in on myself.
Instead I wrap myself around myself
not just in consolation but to fortify that which is
determined to get bigger.
There is no thought of what has grown before me
I am not encumbered by comparison
there is only me and he
and the stretch continues.

– CURRENT PROJECTS FROM –
BRYETTA CALLOWAY

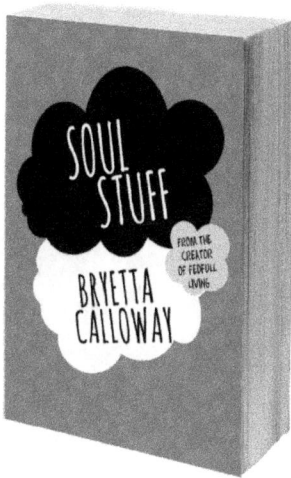

For 45 days, one woman decided to uncensor all the gloriously, messy, raw, and beautifully unbeautiful soul stuff that was bubbling inside. She wrote with no agenda, pouring out the very imaginings of herself. What happened produced a small little book of Soul Stuff she wants to share with you; tears, laughter, and a glimpse into the divine stirrings she muted while living everyday life.

Bryetta Calloway penned Fly Away as an invitation to venture into the timeless questions of love, life, and the time in between. This collection, much like her life, is influenced by Soul, Stage, Jazz, and more. She effortlessly combines her powerfully expressive voice with jazzy vocal posturing to offer lyrical snapshots. A life spent living and performing internationally from Italy to Japan and nationally as well, landed her in the heart of Greenwich Village, NYC. A student at New York University's Tisch School of the Arts, Bryetta began the process of smearing together genres with vintage vocal leanings, standard arrangements, and modern quirk. There is no single style but instead a commitment to music, soul, and song. - www.bryetta.com

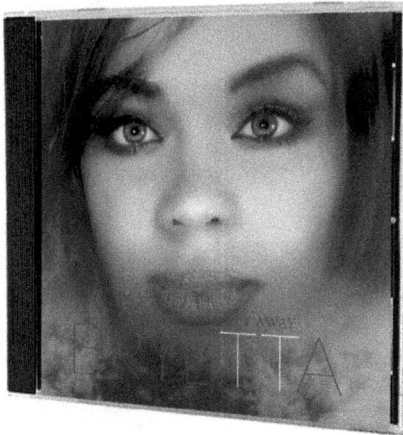

www.ingramcontent.com/pod-product-compliance
Lightning Source LLC
Chambersburg PA
CBHW060014050426
42448CB00012B/2745